Come Sit with Me Once More

Come Sit with Me Once More

SERMONS FOR CHILDREN

Don-Paul Benjamin and Ron Miner

Illustrated by
Don-Paul Benjamin

The Pilgrim Press
New York

Library of Congress Cataloging-in-Publication Data

Benjamin, Don-Paul, 1945–
    Come sit with me once more: sermons for children / Don-Paul
Benjamin and Ron Miner ; illustrated by Don-Paul Benjamin.
        p.   cm.
    ISBN 0-8298-0871-X
    1. Children's sermons.   I. Miner, Ron, 1938– .   II. Title.
BV4315.B355   1990
252'.53—dc20
                                                          90-36845
                                                              CIP

The Pilgrim Press, 475 Riverside Drive, New York, New York 10115

Contents

Preface

"Come sit with me."

For years, this special invitation has been issued to the children of the First Presbyterian Church in Corvallis, Oregon. Recently, a growing number of churches have modified their services of worship to include a joyful moment when the youngsters of the congregation are called forward to experience a special sermon. The increased popularity of such worship activities is, we hope, in some small part due to the success of our first two books. Therefore, we are pleased to offer this, our third collection of sermons for children. We have continued the popular format of our first two books, including both general activities and those focused on major holidays and events.

Acknowledgments

Without the assistance, insistence, and inspiration of many people, this book would not have been possible. Special thanks and love to John Dennis and Erwin Barron. Also to beloved departed parents, Leonard and Carol Benjamin, and Gerald Miner. Finally, special gratitude and love to mother, Alice Miner; wife, Betty Miner; and friend, Sandra Dannenfeldt.

Introduction

In introducing our first two books, we emphasized that the future of the church lies in our younger generation. Children exhibit an exuberance for life and for learning. One has only to observe them in the context of a sermon activity to appreciate the potency of their focused attention and energy.

However, as we developed this, our third book, we were particularly struck with the notion that both children and adults benefit when a service of worship includes sermons for young people. The sense of wonder and curiosity that girls and boys bring to the arena of the children's sermon is inspirational and highly contagious. We have noted with satisfaction that all members of the congregation are influenced by the power of this very special form of active worship. Our observations have been that adults—though seated some distance from the "action"—are in a real sense full participants. Futhermore, their reactions are something more than vicarious; they are empathetic. There must be, in each of us, a desire to be called forward for our own special moment during which we experience the love of God in a truly personal and concrete way. In each adult there must be a child who seeks a basic, nurturing message: that we are unique and special and beloved and that God delights in each of us. For such a message, people of all ages will lean forward and crane their necks to look and listen.

As authors, educators, and Christians, our paths have wound in diverse directions. Ron has remained in Oregon, holding forth Sunday after Sunday with inspirational children's sermons. Don-Paul has relocated to Flagstaff, Arizona, where he continues to write and draw. And yet, when united in our efforts, we evoke a special creative energy. The preparation and delivery of children's sermons continues to influence our lives. We can assure the reader that the marvels of living in loving family environments, among a host of friends, and in the midst of caring congregations are realities which assume new meaning when one is challenged to explain to a child the richness of the Christian experience. This book is devoted to the concept that sermons for children are outgrowths of the natural sharing and learning process which characterizes interactions between children and caring adults. In this sense, the sermons are more than mere shows or presentations. They come from the heart and the intellect, and they project our own sense of wonder.

The children's sermons in this book were adapted from activities that took place on the chancel floor of the First Presbyterian Church in Corvallis, Oregon. The children are called forward about twenty minutes into the service. They sit on the floor with their backs to the congregation, and the leader sits on the floor with them. This establishes a sense of intimacy. A quality hand–held microphone is essential for the success of the sermon activity, because the rest of the congregation can thereby be included. In a few weeks the children become used to speaking into the microphone.

At the end of each sermon are noted "Materials" (needed props) and "Scripture References" (thoughts for meditation) for the leader's use in preparing the sermons. The plan for each sermon includes five basic steps:

1. *Motivation:* A presentation of materials, props, or concepts related to the sermon to set the stage and inspire interest.
2. *Activity:* A tangible experience in which the children can participate. The activity establishes a concrete basis for further discussion.
3. *Guided Discussion:* A period of discussion guided by the leader. Includes key questions for the children to consider and anticipated responses.
4. *Leader Message:* A "script" for the leader with suggested statements. The message is designed to

relate the children's experiences and discussion to Christian life.

5. *Closing Prayer:* A simple prayer that acknowledges the role of God in the topic of the session.

At the end of the sermon, the children may be dismissed to an alternate activity or to return to their families.

There is in the writing of sermons for children an opportunity for us as adults to free the child that dwells inside. We offer these sermons as gifts to the child within each reader.

Ron Miner and Don-Paul Benjamin

Come Sit with Me Once More

Hold Fast

Motivation:
The leader displays two small boards into which some nails have been lightly tapped and some screws firmly imbedded. The screws are holding the two boards together.

Activity:
The children are invited to remove the nails and screws. The leader collects all removed nails.

Guided
Discussion:
You were able to remove the nails, but what about the screws? (They were too tight. Couldn't budge them.) Why are they so hard to get out? (They were screwed in. In too far. They have a different shape. Need a screwdriver to twist them. They have threads.)

Leader
Message:
Yes, these little bits of metal are very special. They are designed to hold fast. When they are in place, they form a firm connection and it is difficult to weaken it. When we join together to worship in our

church, we unite with other Christians and we pledge to hold fast. By uniting together we strengthen our faith. When we join together in our church as Christians, we make a commitment to stick together, to build a strong and solid church.

Closing Prayer:

God, strengthen our faith as we come together to worship. Grant that we may hold fast and share our strength with others. Forgive us when we weaken. We place our trust in you. Amen.

Materials:

Two small wooden boards. A few nails and a few wood screws. Make certain the nails are only lightly tapped in so that small hands can easily remove them. Nails might be blunted before tapping them in. It might be best to countersink the screw heads or to use roundheaded wood screws so that no sharp corners are exposed to injure fingers. Make certain the points of the screws do not protrude from the opposite side of the board.

Scripture Reference:

Proverbs 4:4

Go Team

Motivation: The leader invites several church workers to come forward, each wearing a matching shirt or uniform top.

Activity: The children are invited to meet these people and find out what each one does at the church. After a brief period of interaction, the leader thanks the guests and, as they depart, assembles the children for the discussion.

Guided
Discussion: What kind of church jobs do these people do? (Various: church secretary, custodian, choir director, education director, youth leader, and so forth.) Why do you think they were all dressed alike? (All work together. All are part of the same team.)

Leader
Message: All of these people and several others
             work together to help our church succeed.
             Even though they don't always wear the
             same uniform, they are still part of a very
             important team, and things just wouldn't
             be the same without them. Let's have
             them all come out again, and let's join
             together with the members of the con-
             gregation in applauding these very special
             workers and all the others they represent.

Closing
Prayer: God, we are made stronger by being part
             of your team. We appreciate the help that
             team members give to one another. We
             treasure also your guidance and support.
             Remind us that we are all part of many
             important teams working to spread the
             good news of your love. Amen.

Materials: Matching shirts for workers to wear. A
             local T-shirt emblem shop is a good
             source. Each shirt might have the name of
             the church and/or the individual's name
             printed on it.

Scripture
Reference: Romans 12:4, 5

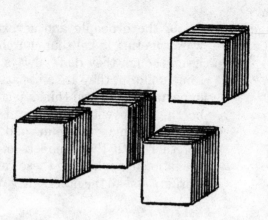

Block Party

Motivation: The leader displays several wooden blocks, all the same size and shape.

Activity: The children are each invited to choose a block. Then each is directed to add a block to a structure which is partially assembled on a platform or table. Their goal is to add each block in such a way that a solid structure will result.

Guided
Discussion: What have we made with our blocks? (Various answers depending on the resulting shape. Typical answers: a house, a building, a wall.) Can you still see the block you added to our structure? (Yes.)

Leader
Message: Our church is a very special structure, and it was built much as we built our block

house [building, wall] today: one piece at a time. Important things are built that way. Now, I want you to take a look at the people in our congregation. Each of them is an important part of our church. Each member of our congregation is like a building block, and together they form the solid structure that is our church.

Closing
Prayer: Remind us, Lord God, that we are part of families, churches, and friendships. Each of these special relationships is like a building block strengthening our lives. Thank you for the strength we feel when we join with others, and especially for our church composed of so many different and special people who care. Amen.

Materials: Wooden blocks and a table or platform. The blocks should be uniform. The platform should be solid and wide enough that children will not have to place blocks in precarious positions. If a solid foundation is constructed on the table or platform using additional blocks, the children will have a good guide for safely placing their own blocks. Keeping the structure low and wide at the base will discourage building a higher structure which might topple over.

Scripture
Reference: 1 Corinthians 12:12b–13a

Birthday Basics

Motivation:	The leader displays a single birthday candle.
Activity:	The children are invited to think about what, in addition to this candle, would be needed to make a child's first birthday party successful.
Guided Discussion:	What is needed to make a successful birthday party? (A cake. Ice cream. Presents. Guests. Games. Party hats and napkins. Invitations.)
Leader Message:	When you think about it, there are only a few simple, basic things needed to make a good birthday party. In fact, all you really need is someone to have the birthday, some guests, and some gifts. Cake and ice

cream and candles are nice, but they aren't absolutely needed. Today [this week, this month] we are celebrating a very special birthday. Today, our church is (number) years old. Now, we don't have all the birthday party items you mentioned, but we do have the basic things: we have our church, we have the guests (indicating children and entire congregation), and we have have some gifts. [At this signal, assistants come forward with a few prearranged gifts which are described to the children.] Let's all stand and sing "Happy Birthday" to our church. [Congregation and choir may join in.]

Closing
Prayer:

Dear God, thank you for our wonderful church. We ask your blessing on all those who serve this church and all who worship here. Amen.

Materials:

A birthday candle. Various prearranged gifts to be presented as part of the church anniversary: new books for the library, new hymnals, new chairs, and so on. Gifts might be the result of fundraising efforts by the congregation. Singing "Happy Birthday" is, of course, performed at the leader's discretion in keeping with the decorum of the sanctuary.

*Scripture
Reference:*

Revelation 22:5b

Huddle Up

Motivation: The leader displays a football.

Activity: [The children are invited to listen and act as the leader takes them through the following activity.] Today we're going to play part of a pretend game of football. First I want you all to line up. [Leader has children line up, shoulder to shoulder, facing the congregation.] Good. Now let's have a huddle. [The leader joins the children in a huddle and gives the following instructions.] Here's the play. When we break the huddle, I want you all to form a line again. Then I'll count to three. When I say, "Three," I want you all to have a seat as we usually do, and we'll have a discussion. Ready? OK let's go! [Children form their line. The leader counts to three and the children reassemble for the discussion.]

Guided Discussion: Why do football players have a huddle? (To learn the play. To talk over what they're going to do. To get instructions. To get the play right so everyone knows what to do and where to go.)

Leader
Message: A huddle is one of the most important
               parts of a football game. When football
               players huddle, they talk over what will
               happen next. They make certain everyone
               knows what to do and where to go. They
               have a huddle so everyone will be pre-
               pared and do his or her best job. It's like
               being a Christian. We prepare ourselves
               to do our very best by attending church
               and going to church school and Bible
               study. We all work hard to learn our parts
               so that when the time comes for action,
               we are all ready, willing, and able to be
               good Christians.

Closing
Prayer: God, thank you for the wonderful lessons
               you provide to help us prepare for our
               Christian life. We look forward with joy to
               learning more and more in church, in
               church school, and in our Bible classes.
               Amen.

Materials: A football. This sermon is best with a
               small group. If the group is large, the
               leader may want to divide the children
               into two teams, each of which forms a
               huddle. By moving back and forth be-
               tween the two huddles, the leader can
               convey the same instructions so that when
               the leader counts to three, the entire
               group is reassembled and ready for the
               discussion.

Scripture
Reference: Matthew 5: 1a; 8:1

Hold the Phone

Motivation: The leader displays two telephones: one is obviously a toy, the other a real phone.

Activity: The children are invited to examine and compare the phones.

Guided Discussion: How are these phones different? (One is a real phone. The other is a toy. One is a fake. Not real.) Which phone would you use to make a call to your family? (The real one.) What is the toy phone good for? (Playing. Pretending.)

Leader Message: Only one of these phones is a real phone. It wasn't too hard to tell the real one. If there was any doubt about which phone was real, all we would have to do is hook them both up and see which one works.

The real one would give us lots of clues. If we picked it up and listened, we'd be able to hear a dial tone. We could call someone and talk to him or her and listen when the person talked back. We could hang up the phone and listen for it to ring. There are many ways to find out if a phone is real, and most of them involve listening. When we listen carefully, we find out all sorts of things. When we listen in church, we hear many wonderful things: we hear singing, and music, and we hear people talking about God. And all these wonderful things make church a very special place where listening is rewarded over and over again.

Closing
Prayer:

Dear God, grant that as we worship together we may truly listen to the reality of your word. Grant that we may listen not only with our ears, but with our hearts as well. Amen.

Materials: A toy phone and a real phone.

*Scripture
Reference:*   Mark 9:7b

In the Bag

Motivation: The leader arrives empty-handed.

Activity: Explaining that the things for today's sermon were left behind, the leader asks an assistant to take four or five children to a nearby corner and have them help carry the needed props back. The children accompany the assistant to a spot where three or four seemingly identical sealed bags are stored. In reality, one of the bags is much heavier than the others. The assistant gives one light bag each to individual children, but has two or three children jointly carry the heavier one. When all have arrived, the leader begins the discussion.

Guided
Discussion: Do you think all these bags contain the same thing? (No.) Why not? (One was heavier. The others were light.) How many people did it take to carry the heavy bag? (Two or three.)

Leader
Message: All the light bags [open one to demonstrate] contain tissue paper. They are very light and easily handled by one person. This bag [open to demonstrate] contains rocks. It is heavy and needed a team to carry it. You couldn't really tell from the outside. All these bags seemed to be the same until it came time to lift them. Then it was clear that one was heavier than the others. Now, when we see people, we are often unaware that they too are carrying heavy burdens. They may be lonely or tired or sick. They may be sad or angry or lost. They may be upset about work. They may be poor. They may be worried. But though they may feel bad on the inside, we can't really tell by looking at them from the outside. Each of us has problems and concerns that we must carry. But we don't need to carry them alone. Others can help us and we can help others. And, together, we can also seek help from God.

Closing
Prayer: Thank you, God, for your help and for the help of others. We bring our burdens, large and small, to you. Grant that we may help others even as we pray to you for assistance. Amen.

Materials:	Three or four identical bags (cloth ones if possible, but sturdy paper bags will do). When sealed, the bags should all appear to be approximately the same size and shape. All bags but one should be filled with tissue paper. One bag should be filled with rocks or other heavy objects, though not too heavy to be lifted and carried a short distance by two or three children. The bags should be sturdy enough to ensure that the bottoms will not break under the weight of the rocks or other heavy material. As a precaution, the assistant might make certain to give the heavy bag to larger, older children and may even lend a hand in carrying the load so as to guard against the bag or objects inside being accidently dropped on the children's feet.
Scripture Reference:	Galatians 6:2

Peanut Butter and Jelly

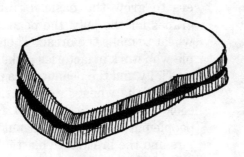

Motivation:	The leader arrives and walks to a table on which are a jar of peanut butter, a jar of jelly, a knife, and two slices of bread.
Activity:	As the children watch, the leader proceeds to make a peanut butter and jelly sandwich. When this task is complete, assistants remove the materials and the leader joins the children for the discussion.
Guided Discussion:	I have a riddle: How many people does it take to make a peanut butter and jelly sandwich? (One.) Well, it's true I made a sandwich just now, but who made the bread? (A baker. The grocery store person.) Yes, and who made the peanut butter? (A factory worker. A cook.) How about the jelly? (A farmer. A factory worker. A cook.)

Leader	
Message:	When you think about it, you realize that it takes several people to make a peanut butter and jelly sandwich. It takes farmers to grow the basic ingredients: the grapes for the jelly, the peanuts, and the wheat to make the bread. Then other people who work in factories make the grapes into jelly and the peanuts into peanut butter and the wheat into flour. Meanwhile, cooks have to bake the bread. Next, other people put the jelly and peanut butter into jars and the bread into plastic bags. Then still other people load the jars and the loaves of bread onto trucks. And other people unload them and put them onto shelves in the store. Then someone buys them, and finally they end up in my hands so I can make a sandwich. I may have even left some people out, but you get the idea: it takes many, many people working together to make something happen. You know, in order for our church to operate, many people have to work long and hard. Today we are going to honor some of those people, some people all of you know—our church school teachers. [At this signal, the teachers come forward and an appropriate ceremony ensues. Following the closing prayer, the children and teachers leave together, possibly to go to a special sharing time in the church school.]
Closing	
Prayer:	Dear God, thank you for these wonderful helpers. Bless them for their unselfish work on behalf of our church. Amen.

Materials: A table. A jar of peanut butter and a jar of jelly. Two slices of bread. A table knife. So that the children won't feel cheated, it might be possible to arrange for them to partake of peanut butter and jelly sandwiches when they retire, with their teachers, to the church school. Naturally, dietary restrictions should be honored and alternative food available as needed. Although church school teachers are the focus of this sermon, other workers could be honored (kitchen staff, choir, and so forth) with some slight alterations in the Leader Message.

Scripture
Reference: Deuteronomy 6:5–7a

Kaleidoscopic Congregation

Motivation: The leader produces a kaleidoscope and an ordinary cardboard tube.

Activity: The children are invited to look through each of these objects.

Guided Discussion: What did you see through the kaleidoscope? (Colors. Neat shapes. Pretty things.) What did you see through the tube? (Nothing. Just the church. People. Uninteresting things.)

Leader Message: Think for a moment about what it would be like if you were a new person visiting our church. Before you came inside, you might look at our stained glass windows and think how pretty they looked. (See "Materials" for suggestions if your church does not have stained glass windows.) Looking at our church from the outside is sort of like looking through this kaleidoscope. It looks very pretty and a little mysterious. Once a new person was inside our church, however, things might not look the same. The person might look around, just as you looked through this plain tube, and decide that this is, after all, just a building and that we are all just people and that maybe this isn't the special place he or she has been looking for. How can we change that impression? How can we make new people feel the power and beauty of this special place which is our church? Here's the answer [leader holds the plain tube up to his or her eye and looks toward the congregation]. When I look through this tube, I see a wonderful kaleidoscope of people. I see our colorful, lively, caring, and loving congregation. What we can all do when new people come to visit is to share our love and enthusiasm so they too will see this church as we see it: a loving and wonderful place to worship God.

Closing
Prayer: Thank you, God, for guiding visitors our way. Grant that we may impress them with our love and caring so that, through us, they may come to know you. Amen.

Materials: A kaleidoscope and a plain tube. Depending on the number of children, it may be difficult to have every child take a turn looking through each instrument. If possible, the leader may want to have more than one of each available, or volunteers may be chosen to do the viewing. It is best, however, if all children can look through one or the other so that they can contribute to the discussion and more readily relate to the message. If, as is often true in our modern society, the leader's church is not an established sanctuary complete with stained glass windows, the sermon can be modified as follows: The activity can proceed as written. The leader message can be adapted so that the visitor's view through the kaleidoscope becomes that person's *expectation* of what the church will look like and the view through the tube can be the visitor's *disappointment* with what he or she perceives to be the church's limitations.

Scripture
Reference: Psalm 84:1

Promises to Keep

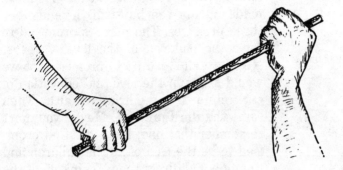

Motivation: The leader displays a long, flexible stick.

Activity: The leader places the stick on the floor and invites various children to come to one end and try to pick up the stick.

Guided
Discussion: Picking up that stick was no easy task. What would have made it easier? (If the stick had been shorter. If we had had help. Someone at the other end.) Yes, it would have helped a lot to have had someone holding up the other end. [If the point of having someone hold up the other end of the stick does not emerge in the discussion, the leader can provide a demonstration by holding one end while a volunteer holds the other.]

Leader
Message: Did you ever hear someone use the words "holding up your end"? We often use such words when we make an agreement with someone. We say, "I'll hold up my end of the bargain if you hold up your end." Then

we promise each other that we will each do our part. Today we heard promises made during the baptism. I remember three promises: The pare..cs promised to raise the children in the love of Jesus. Next, we all stood up to promise that we would share in the love and education of each child in the Christian faith. Then came the third promise. Maybe you don't remember that one, but I do. God promised to be the God of all the children and to guide and direct them. Think of all the wonderful help these children will have as they grow!

Closing
Prayer:

Dear God, sometimes we make promises that are hard to keep. We ask your help. And we pray that we may help others to be true to their promises. We know you will hold up your end; help us to hold up ours. Thank you for being with us always. Amen.

Materials:

A long, thin, flexible stick or board. It will be best to position the activity so that the board will not cause damage if it wriggles about when the children try to lift it. Obviously, the content of the Leader Message will vary depending upon the nature of the baptism ceremony and whether infants, children, or adults are baptized.

Scripture
Reference: Galatians 3:14b

Water, Water, Everywhere

Motivation: The leader displays a plastic pitcher of water and a clear plastic bowl.

Activity: The children are invited to watch and listen as the leader carefully fills the bowl with water.

Guided Discussion: What does water feel like? (Wet. Cold. Nice. Refreshing.) What does water sound like? (Like a waterfall. Like gurgling. Like a river.) What can we do with water? (Swim in it. Water plants. Take a bath. Wash the car. Drink it. Mix it with things to cook and eat. Go fishing. Go boating. Water ski.)

Leader Message: It is difficult, isn't it, to talk about what water is like. Water feels like water. It sounds like water. It looks like water. Water is water. But when it comes to uses for water, we have lots of ideas. Water is extremely useful. Not only that, water is absolutely required for life. Without water, there would be no plants, no rivers, no lakes, no oceans, and no living things. Without water, there would be nothing. This precious liquid has many uses, including the one we witnessed [are about to witness] today: baptism. When we use water in the baptism ceremony we are using it to symbolize a rebirth, a cleansing of the person who is baptized. In baptism, water is a symbol, not only of life, but of new life. Baptism is a very important beginning which makes a very special use of water, the liquid of life.

Closing
Prayer:

Dear God, thank you for the joy of baptism. Thank you for the rebirth and cleansing symbolized by water, your precious resource. Amen.

Materials:

A plastic pitcher filled with water. A clear plastic bowl. Plastic is suggested for safety reasons. If the bowl is clear, the effect of pouring the water will be dramatized for the children. Once the activity demonstration has concluded, the materials should be put out of reach to avoid spills. It might be effective if the water and utensils used in this sermon could also be used in the baptism ceremony.

*Scripture
Reference:*

Revelation 7:17

Sink Thinking

Motivation: The leader displays an old bathroom sink.

Activity: The children are invited to examine the
                sink.

Guided
Discussion: What is this? (A sink. A bathroom sink.)
                What do you use a bathroom sink for?
                (Washing. Brushing teeth. Getting a
                drink.) Could we wash our hands in this
                sink? (No.) Why not? (No water coming
                in. No pipes going out.)

Leader
Message: That's right. Without pipes this sink is not
                much good. It needs connections. We are
                like this sink. We need connections too.
                We need something coming in and some-
                thing going out. We need God's love com-

ing in, we need it flowing around and through us, and we need to let it flow out again to others. One of the very best ways to make the connections we need is through prayer. Let's pray together.

Closing
Prayer: Thank you, God, for the connections in our lives. We are connected to our families and to our church. In order to be whole, we need to be connected to you and to the love and support of those around us. Amen.

Materials: A small bathroom sink with no pipes. It might help children identify it if the faucets are in place.

Scripture
Reference: Isaiah 12:3

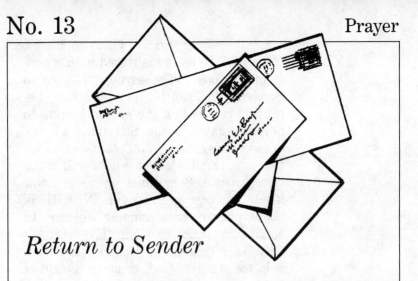

Return to Sender

Motivation: The leader displays a stack of used envelopes (bills, personal letters, advertisements, and so forth). Each envelope has a
canceled stamp and return address.

Activity: The children are invited to examine the
envelopes as the leader passes them
among the group.

Guided
Discussion: What do you see here? (Bills. Letters.
Envelopes. Advertisements. Stamps.)

Leader
Message: It is interesting that before I open a letter,
I often look first to see who sent it. I can
tell this by looking in the upper left-hand
corner of the envelope for the return address. We put a return address on the
mail we send so whoever receives it will
know it's from us and so the post office can
return it to us if, for some reason, it can-
not be properly delivered. Sometimes, if I
make a mistake on an address, my letters

come back to me undelivered with a note from the post office saying, "Return to Sender." This can be very upsetting, because it means that the person I wrote to never got my message. So sending a letter doesn't always work. Not often, but sometimes, the mail is lost or is delivered to the wrong house. Sometimes we never know if our message got through. Now, think about prayer for a minute. We pray to send a message to God: "Everything's OK, God. Thank you, God. Please, God, help me. Please, God, come to the aid of my family or my friends. Help me decide what to do, God." Do those messages get through? Our faith tells us yes. Our faith is that our letters to God—our prayers—are always delivered.

Closing
Prayer:
Dear God, thank you for receiving our prayers. Amen.

Materials:
A collection of canceled envelopes (ideally without letters inside), all of which have return addresses. A variety will be useful, including personal mail, bills, and advertisements.

*Scripture
Reference:*
1 John 1:5

Music Magic

Motivation and Activity: After the children have been called forward, a violinist appears and plays a brief melody, ideally a duet with a member of the choir in which voice and instrument take turns echoing each other. The leader and children applaud and the musicians exit.

Guided Discussion: Does anyone recognize that musical instrument? (Violin.) What does the sound of a violin remind you of? (Various answers. Sadness or other emotions. A cat. A bird. A person singing.)

Leader Message:  A stringed instrument such as a violin is considered very special because it often reminds people of the human voice. As people, we use our voices for many things: to talk on the telephone, to shout at a basketball game, to sing. But I think the human voice is most beautiful when it is used in prayer. You may recall that there are stringed instruments mentioned in the Bible. The harp and the lyre, for instance, were often used to accompany those who sang the psalms. From now on, when you pray, think of your words as beautiful music floating to Jesus and to God. [At this point, the soloist, the violinist, and the choir might combine to perform the Lord's Prayer or a psalm with the congregation, and the children invited to join in.]

Closing
Prayer:

Lord's Prayer (sung) or, Dear God, thank you for the power and the beauty of prayer. Amen.

Materials:

A violinist, or other musician playing a cello, viola, or other stringed instrument. If such a performer is unavailable, a pianist or organist or a reed player may be substituted. If the instrumental soloist can perform a duet with a vocal soloist, the similarity between the instrument and the voice will be more apparent to the children. The leader should confer with the church's music director for suggestions and assistance.

*Scripture
Reference:*

Psalm 150:1, 4a

Wake-up Call

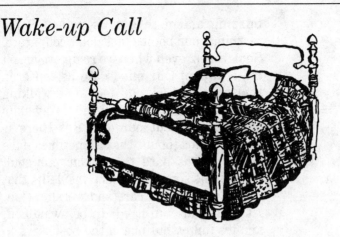

Motivation: The leader, carrying a pillow and a blanket, joins the group.

Activity: As the children watch, the leader makes a comfy bed, lies down, and pretends to sleep. After a short period (probably attended by much giggling) the leader "wakes up," puts the bedding aside, and questions the children.

Guided Discussion: Do you like to sleep? (Yes.) So do I. Of course, there is a time and place for sleep, but even when we go to bed on time it's hard sometimes to wake up. Who wakes you up at your house? (My mom. Dad. Brother. Sister. Alarm clock.) Do you always get up right away when you are called? (Yes. No.)

Leader Message: Sometimes it takes a lot to wake us up. Some of us really like to stay in bed. It may take several reminders, or a loud buzzing alarm to get us going. Some mornings our bodies just don't cooperate. Sometimes, even when we're up, we aren't quite awake. Our minds are asleep even though we're on our feet and walking around. Eventually, our minds awaken and we go about our day. But there is another part of us that sometimes falls asleep and is hard to awaken: our soul. Our soul is something deep inside us that makes us love and care and worship God. At times our soul needs to be awakened, and it's funny, but one of the best ways to wake up a soul is not with loud noises or repeated calling. The soul often responds to something much different, to something very much like silence—something called *meditation*. The most powerful wake-up call our soul can receive is quiet, a quiet during which we can think deeply about God. Let's all join the congregation in a powerful moment of quiet meditation. [After a short silence, the leader closes with the prayer.]

Closing
Prayer:

Dear God, we thank you for special moments of quiet that enrich our souls. (Pause for a moment of quiet.) Amen.

Materials: A pillow and a blanket.

Scripture
Reference: Psalm 46:10a

A Tale of Nails

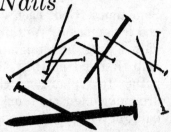

Motivation: The leader displays a clear plastic jar containing a variety of nails of different sizes and metals.

Activity: The leader passes the jar from child to child and invites each to examine the nails inside.

Guided Discussion: Let's talk about nails. Pretend you had just one nail. What could you do with one nail? (Nail two boards together. Pound it into something. Put up a picture on the wall.) What could you do with two nails? (Nail more boards together. Hang two pictures.) What could you do with a hundred nails? (Build a wall. Build a house.)

Leader Message: The more nails we have, the more things we can build. Each nail is like a gift a person gives to our church. Some people give money, some give time, some give their talents, and all give their love. Each of these gifts helps build things—not only buildings and rooms, but things like trust and love. The more gifts we receive, the more things we can build.

Closing	
Prayer:	Sometimes, God, each of us feels small and insignificant. We think that our individual gifts and talents can't possibly help. Remind us that when we join together to support our church, our gifts are multiplied. Let us, like individual nails, be a force to hold our church and our world together. Amen.
Materials:	A clear plastic (unbreakable) jar containing nails of various metals and sizes.
Scripture *Reference:*	1 Corinthians 12:4

Picture This

Motivation: The leader displays a baby picture.

Activity: The picture is passed among the children
                  and back to the leader.

Guided
Discussion: What are some of the ways babies change?
                  (They get bigger. Grow up. Begin to
                  walk.) Who do you think this baby is?
                  (Various guesses.)

Leader
Message: I am the baby in the picture. I have
                  changed quite a bit since that picture was
                  taken. Just think of how much you have
                  changed since you were a baby. As we
                  grow and change, we have many new ad-
                  ventures, and with each passing year we
                  learn more and more. When I was little, I
                  spoke like a baby and I saw things like a
                  baby. Now that I have grown, I speak

differently and I see things differently. My early words and my early thoughts have grown just as my body has grown. When I first thought about God, I couldn't quite understand. As I have grown and learned more, I understand more and more. And I have found that the church helps me learn. I look forward, as I hope all of you do, to living and growing and learning more about God.

Closing Prayer: Dear God, you loved us as babies and continue to love us as we grow and change. Be with us always and care for us as we grow in our ability to know and serve you. Surround us with your love as we grow in our knowledge of you. Amen.

Materials: A baby picture of the leader.

Scripture Reference: 1 Corinthians 13:11

Pump Up

Motivation: The leader displays a very flat football and a hand pump.

Activity: The leader hands the football to a child.

Guided Discussion: Is this football ready to use? (No.) Why not? (The ball is flat.) What does it need? (It needs to be pumped up. Needs air.) Let's try to fix it. [The leader holds the hand pump a distance from the football and pumps.] Nothing happened. Why isn't it filling with air? (Have to get closer. Have to hook it up to the ball. Have to get them together.) [Using this advice, the leader properly inflates the football.]

Leader Message: Air is all around us. Even though we can't see it, we know it is there. When we need air, we just breathe and the air flows in. That works for people and for animals, and to a certain extent it works for plants too. It doesn't work for things like footballs or tires or inner tubes or balloons. We have to make some kind of connection to supply air to these things. We have to get close and send the air their way. Love is a little like air. As Christians we feel love all around us, especially in church.

When we need love, we just open our hearts and the love flows in. That works for us, but we need to remember that there are others outside our church who don't feel the love. We need to get close to these people and send love their way. Just as the pump allows us to send air to this football, we need to let God's love flow through us to others.

Closing Prayer:

Thank you, God, for the love and beauty that surrounds us. Like the air we breathe, your love is essential. When your love enters our lives we grow and thrive. Help us to direct your love into the lives of people around us. Amen.

Materials:

A deflated football and a hand pump with a needle used to inflate sports equipment. If a sport other than football is in season, a different ball may be used. The same effect may also be obtained by using a small inner tube or an inflatable beach ball. The leader should be careful, however, not to choose an object that will take an inordinate amount of time to inflate by hand.

Scripture Reference:

Acts 2:4

No Stone Unturned

Motivation:	The leader displays a collection of smooth pebbles and rough stones.
Activity:	The pebbles and stones are passed from child to child.
Guided Discussion:	What can you tell me about these stones? (Various answers related to size, shape, color, and so forth. They are hard. Some are smooth and some are rough.)
Leader Message:	Stones are interesting. The stones we have examined today are in many ways just ordinary stones. But, as you noticed, some of them are rough and some are very smooth. The rough stones are from high in the mountains where the cold, cold winters and the hot summers cause large cliffs to split into small, jagged pieces, something like the way glass breaks. The smooth pebbles are from the banks of a river [or a seashore]. These have been worn smooth by the action of the water and sand moving over and over them, wearing them smooth in somewhat the same way sandpaper wears down a piece of wood. You know, people are interesting too. Some are rough and some are smooth. Rough people are often angry.

They talk loudly and say mean things. Smooth people smile a lot and are kind. What makes the difference, I wonder, in the way smooth people live their lives? Well, unlike stones, people have something inside. If you look inside a stone, you'll find more stone. If you look inside a person, you'll find a soul. Everyone has one, even rough people. I like to think it's possible that, unlike rocks which are made rough or smooth by forces from the outside, people are made rougher or smoother by forces from the inside. It's not the life they live or how life treats them that makes people rough or smooth, it's the strength of God's love they have inside.

Closing Prayer:

God, thank you for the strength we have inside. Help us to gather courage to face the challenges the world sends our way without becoming rough. Help us to show others our smooth side. Amen.

Materials:

Two sets of stones: rough and smooth. The rough stones should not be so coarse as to injure the children's hands, but they must be rough enough to provide a contrast with the smoother pebbles. Pebbles can be obtained from a nearby riverbank or ocean shore, or—if this is impractical—from a local hobby or souvenir shop. Rougher stones might be obtained from a gravel road since the road-making process often yields rugged nuggets.

Scripture Reference: Luke 3:5

Kite Kit

Motivation:	The leader displays an unassembled kite: string, sticks, and paper.
Activity:	The children are invited to examine these materials and to be prepared to tell how they can be used to make something.
Guided Discussion:	What can be make with these items? (A kite.) Can we fly our kite indoors? (No.) Why not? (Need room. Need the sky. It would get tangled inside. Would hit the ceiling. Need wind.)
Leader Message:	Without wind, a kite is just a collection of string, paper, and sticks. It is when the kite is caught up in the wind that it truly

becomes a kite. Let's talk about the wind. Can you see the wind? (Various answers about seeing branches blow, leaves floating on the breeze, and so on. Most will agree that the wind itself is unseen.) Although we can see the wind in action as it blows things around, including kites, we really can't see the wind itself. We can feel the wind and we can hear it, but we can't see it. The wind is a little like God's love. We can feel God's love and we can hear it in the voices of our families and in the hymns we sing in church. We can even see the way God's love affects people. We can see how it makes them confident and joyful and good. But we can't really see God's love even though our faith tells us how very, very real that love is. We are like kites. We are lifted higher and held up by our faith in the unseen wonder of God's love.

Closing
Prayer:
Dear God, we thank you for your unseen, overpowering love. Thank you for lifting us to new heights. We soar like kites lifted by the strength of your wonderful love. Amen.

Materials:
An unassembled kite: string, sticks, and paper.

Scripture
Reference:
Isaiah 40:31

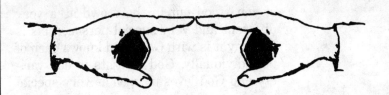

Follow the Leader

Motivation:	The leader invites the children to stand side by side in a row facing the congregation. The leader then takes a position opposite the center of the children's row. The leader faces toward the children, away from the congregation.
Activity:	[The children are invited to follow along as the leader demonstrates various movements.] Do as I do. Can you snap your fingers? Twiddle your thumbs? Shut your eyes and touch your nose? Open your eyes and pat your head and rub your tummy at the same time? Reach up high? Stand on tiptoe? [After leading the children through a variety of movements, the leader has the children sit down again.]
Guided Discussion:	What did you notice as we went through our movements? (It was fun. Some people got mixed up. I couldn't do some things.)
Leader Message:	Even though you all listened carefully and tried to do the same things, we each did them differently. Each of you acted in a very special way. No two were alike. Each

of you stood out in the crowd as a very different and very special person. This is the way it is with God. God knows each of us individually. God delights in our variety and God loves us each as very special people.

Closing
Prayer:

God, our Creator, you have given us being. You have made us each unique and special. We are each as precious and special to you as these children are to our church. Thank you for caring for us and for giving us the gift of life. Amen.

Materials:

If the leader feels the children will be distracted or embarrassed by facing the congregation during the activity, the directions in which the leader and the children face, respectively, can be reversed. For some groups, it might be more effective to have the children just remain in their usual places while the leader conducts the activity. This approach may discourage more demonstrative children from putting on a show for the congregation.

Scripture
Reference:

Psalm 139:1

Up, Up, and Away

Motivation: The leader displays a large helium-filled balloon that is tethered by multiple strings to a length of wood.

Activity: The children are invited to examine this arrangement and to be prepared to discuss it.

Guided
Discussion: Why do you suppose I have tied this balloon down like this? (To hold it down. So it won't float away. So you won't lose it.) Why did I use so many strings? (It's a big balloon.)

Leader
Message: Like this balloon, people want to be free, but they are held down by bad deeds and bad thoughts. Jesus has promised that our love for God can set us free. Our love for God can cut the strings that hold us down and allow our lives to rise higher and higher. Maybe you'd like a demonstration. [The leader produces a pair of scissors and snips each string in succession.] Let's release ourselves from the burden of lying. [Snip one string.] Let's stop fighting. [Snip one string.] No more sin. [Snip one string.] Away with loving ourselves more than others. [Snip.] Let's end hatred. [Snip.] [At the final snip, the balloon floats freely away.]

Closing
Prayer: God, you lift us higher. Thank you for showing us the way to cut the strings that hold us down. Grant that we may come to you freely and with trust in your word. Amen.

Materials: A large helium-filled balloon. Strings of varying lengths. A length of board. A pair of scissors. The message will be enhanced if the leader cuts first the shortest string, then the next shortest, and so on. In this way, the balloon will lurch upward with each snip, only to be pulled up short by the next longest string. This will contribute to the anticipation of the balloon's eventual release. The phrases that accompany the snipping can, of course, be modified as the leader desires. This activity can be accomplished either in or out of doors. Giving the sermon outdoors on a warm day—perhaps as part of a special outdoor service of worship—would be quite effective. If indoors, the leader should make certain that the rising balloon will not burst on the ceiling or on a light fixture. A disadvantage to doing the activity indoors is that the balloon will continue to hover as a distraction for the rest of the service. Therefore, if performed indoors, the activity might best be left until the end of the regular service. This entire procedure should be rehearsed by the leader to ensure that the balloon has sufficient buoyancy to rise with all strings attached. Using a large balloon will help. Remember that temperature affects helium, in that cold may inhibit the balloon's ascent. Cutting the strings in such a way that only a small portion of string remains attached to the balloon with each snip will help reduce the weight the balloon must eventually carry.

Scripture Reference: Romans 8:2

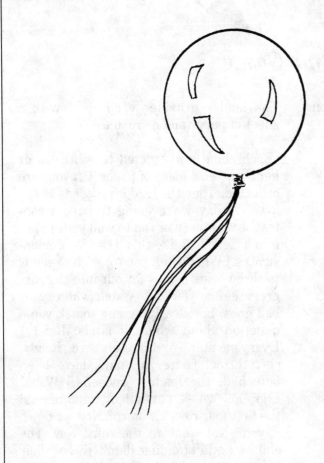

A Name Game

Motivation: The leader provides each child with a sheet of paper and a crayon.

Activity: [Each child is instructed to write his or her name on a piece of paper. Crayons are collected. Then the leader proceeds as follows.] Today we're going to have a contest! I want each of you to wad your paper into a tight ball like this. [Leader demonstrates.] When I tell you to, each of you is to throw your ball as far out into the congregation as you can. Watch where your ball goes, because I'm going to ask you a question about where it lands. Ready? Everyone stand and line up here. Ready, set, throw! [After all balls have been launched, the leader proceeds.] Would everyone whose paper ball went beyond the first four rows sit down? Now sit down if your ball went to the third row. The children still standing didn't throw their balls very far, did they? I want everyone, including the congregation, to give the children still standing a big round of applause. [The leader leads the children and the congregation in applauding those who "threw short." Then the leader has all the children sit down.]

Guided
Discussion:

What did you think of that contest? (It was wierd. The best throwers didn't get applause.) Whom did we all clap and cheer for? (The people who didn't throw very far.)

Leader
Message:

Usually we celebrate the best throw or the highest jump or the one who gets most points. We cheer and clap for people who win, the ones who come in first. Somehow it doesn't seem fair to reward the ones who finish last. Jesus was aware of our human tendency to celebrate the winners and say to the losers, "Better luck next time." Jesus wanted to remind us that everyone who loves God is a winner whether or not that person is first or last in the eyes of other people. He said that the first shall be last and the last shall be first. By that Jesus meant that we are all important to God.

Closing
Prayer:

God, we're so grateful that you love us even when we're not number one. We celebrate the fact that you accept each of us and love us in spite of our shortcomings and even in spite of our accomplishments. Amen.

Materials: Pieces of paper and crayons, and perhaps a writing surface of some kind. Care should be taken that the carpet or floor is not marred during the activity, since crayons may poke holes in paper when wielded by small hands. If it is felt that throwing paper balls toward the congregation may be too disruptive or rude, or that the children will have trouble with the concept of how many rows their throw encompassed, the leader may wish to have the children throw on a "field" or "course" constructed by using string or tape to indicate distance. Children are asked to write their names, to reinforce "ownership", making it more likely they will watch where the wads go. The leader may wish to substitute some other type of contest in which losers are rewarded. However, this activity has the advantage of being relatively safe plus being sufficiently innoccuous so that "winners" will not get upset when their accomplishments (such as they are) are ignored.

Scripture
Reference: Matthew 20:14b–16

Food for the Soul

Motivation: The leader displays a variety of seeds and plants.

Activity: Each child is invited to examine these items and decide what they are.

Guided
Discussion: What are these things? (Some are seeds. Nuts. Leaves. Branches. Food. That's an olive.)

Leader
Message: I brought all these things to show you for a very special reason. Everything you see here is mentioned in the Bible. Often one or more of these things was mentioned by Jesus in a parable. A parable is a short story that contains a lesson. For example, Jesus told a parable about a fig tree, a tree with big green leaves that bears fruit like this [indicating a fig]. Jesus also mentioned a vineyard, a place where grapes like this one are grown. A mustard seed, like this one [or like the ones used to make this mustard], is also included in one of Jesus' parables. Elsewhere in the Bible, an almond tree is mentioned [indicating the almond]. So are barley, dates, olives, gourds, and lentils. There are many references in the Bible to food and to growing and harvesting and eating. In one par-

able, Jesus told about a large supper, a fine feast to which many people were invited. Maybe some of the very foods you see here were on the table. But when it was time for the meal, the guests all sent excuses saying they couldn't come. The person in charge of the feast was very upset, and soon invitations were issued to a whole new crowd of guests. When the new guests arrived, the person in charge greeted them warmly saying, "Welcome to those of you who accepted my invitation. You are my new guests. Come in and be satisfied. Those who were first invited and would not come will never taste my feast." The Bible is filled with stories about food and filled also with wonderful information about God's love. We can think of the Bible as a feast waiting for us. God invites us, and all who accept that invitation will never go hungry.

Closing
Prayer:

Dear God, thank you for the invitation to join in your feast. Thank you also for the nourishment your word provides. Your love fills us to overflowing. Amen.

Materials:

Various biblical foodstuffs such as figs, grapes, mustard seeds (or mustard), almonds, barley, dates, olives, gourds, and lentils. These might be displayed in plastic bags or other clear containers to facilitate handling and avoid spills.

*Scripture
Reference:*

Luke 14:17

Room to Grow

Motivation: The leader arrives carrying a small suit-
               case.

Activity: As the children watch, the leader opens
               the suitcase and, one by one, removes and
               displays items of baby or toddler clothing
               obviously too small for the children in the
               group.

Guided
Discussion: Do you remember clothes like these?
               (Yes.) When did you wear them? (Years
               ago. When I was little. When I was a
               baby.) What would happen if you tried to
               put them on now? (Too small. They
               wouldn't fit. Would be too tight. Would
               rip.)

Leader
Message: As you grow, the clothes you once wore
               don't fit anymore. Your arms and legs get
               longer and you grow taller and taller. You
               change and you need new things. As you
               grow, your ideas change too. Ideas you
               once had now seem like baby ideas. You
               have grown to have new ideas and to think

new thoughts. The old thoughts don't fit anymore. They are too small. The Bible tells us that Jesus welcomed children: "Let the little children come to me [Matt. 19:14]." These are the words Jesus used. The Bible also tells us that people grow up. When we are children, the Bible says, we think and act like children. Later, as we grow up, our thoughts and actions grow too. As you come to church and learn about and read the Bible, your small thoughts change to bigger and bigger thoughts. In fact, all of us in our church, even though some of us are older, grow bigger and bigger each time we come to worship and each time we consult the Bible. We never stop growing as we learn more and more.

Closing Prayer: Thank you, God, for welcoming us as children and then allowing us to continue to learn and grow through your love. Amen.

Materials: A small suitcase or other container. Various items of baby or toddler clothing that are obviously too small for the children in the group. It is best if the clothing items are "gender neutral," that is, neither obviously girls' nor boys' clothing.

Scripture Reference: 1 Corinthians 13:11

That Sinking Feeling

Motivation: The leader displays two small model
               houses along with a small concrete slab
               and a square of prepared gelatin mix.

Activity: The children are invited to watch as the
               leader carefully places, in turn, a house on
               each "foundation."

Guided
Discussion: What happened? (The house on the gela-
               tin sank. The other one sat firmly in
               place.) Why did the house on the gelatin
               sink? (Bottom/foundation was too flimsy.
               House was too heavy. The gelatin is too
               squishy.)

Leader
Message: Jesus once told a story about two
               builders. One built a house on a solid foun-
               dation, like our concrete, and this house
               was strong and unshakable. The other
               builder, however, did not use a good foun-
               dation, and the house fell and was ruined.
               Jesus said that the first builder—the one
               who used the solid foundation—was like a
               person who hears the word of God and
               does what God says. The life of this good
               listener is strong and solid because it is
               built upon the strong foundation of God's
               word and the listener's action. The builder
               with the weak foundation is like a person
               who hears the word of God, but ignores
               the message. The life of such a person is
               likely to sink lower and lower until it
               comes tumbling down.

Closing Prayer:	Dear God, we thank you for sending Jesus to spread the good news of your word. Grant that we may hear and understand and act according to your word. Amen.
Materials:	Two small model houses. These might be obtained from a toy store or thrift shop. If there is a carpenter in the congregation, this person might be asked to build a couple of small house shapes, using as a guide

the sketch above. A single house could be used for the demonstration, placing it first on the solid foundation and then on the gelatin. If the leader finds obtaining a house too difficult, a wooden block might be substituted. A door and windows drawn on the block can enhance the idea of a house. A piece of cardboard creased in the middle can be glued or taped on top of the block to make a roof. A small slab of concrete or cinder block and a square of prepared gelatin are also needed. The leader should place the gelatin on a large platter to catch the overflow caused by the sinking house. It will probably be best to set up these items ahead of time or to have assistants bring them forward, in the interest of time and convenience.

Scripture Reference:	Luke 6:46–49.

A Shiner

Motivation:	The leader displays two shoes: an old, battered shoe and a similar, but shinier, shoe.
Activity:	The children are invited to examine these two shoes.
Guided Discussion:	[Holding up the old shoe.] Anything wrong with this shoe? (Lots. It's scuffed. Has a hole. Is all wrinkled and cracked. Needs shining. It's dirty.) How about this other one; is it OK? (Yes. Nicer. Shinier.)
Leader Message:	Jesus reminds us that we can become new through faith. We may feel old and worn out and wrinkled and sad like this poor old shoe, but we can be renewed by putting our trust in God and in Jesus. As people, we can get scuffed up by life. We can get

kicked around and bruised. Sometimes we even end up hurting ourselves. If our shoes get too badly damaged, we can throw them away and buy a new pair, or we can clean them up, repair them, and make them shine again. When people are damaged, Jesus invites them to come to God and be made new again.

Closing
Prayer:

God, thank you for the promise of renewal. Jesus invites us to come forward and be made new. We accept that invitation. Amen.

Materials:

A pair of old shoes, one of which has been repaired and polished. If it is not practical to use a pair of shoes, any two shoes can be used providing the old/new contrast between them is apparent.

Scripture
Reference:

2 Corinthians 5:17

A Hill of Beans

Motivation: The leader displays a large plastic jar filled with beans.

Activity: The children are invited to examine the jar and to be prepared to guess the number of beans.

Guided
Discussion: How many beans do you think are in this jar? (Various guesses.)

Leader
Message: You all made good guesses. It is almost impossible to guess how many beans this jar contains. There is one way to be certain how many there are, and that is to count them. But that would take a long time. Since I put these beans in this jar, I know how many there are, and I'm going to tell you. I'm going to ask you to take my word for it. I'm going to ask you to believe what I say without letting you actually sit down and count each and every

bean. I'm going to ask you to have faith in what I say. Is that agreed? (Yes.) Good. There are [exact number] beans in this jar. Do you believe I'm telling the truth? (Yes.) Thank you. Your faith makes me feel good. I feel good that you trust me and believe me. You know, when we pray we often say we have faith in God. This is what we mean when we have faith; we accept God's answers, we accept God's truth, and we believe in God's word.

Closing Prayer:
Dear God, we trust you. We accept your answers, your truth, and your holy word. Thank you for rewarding our faith. Amen.

Materials:
A large transparent plastic jar. Enough dry beans to fill the jar. The leader, of course, will count the beans ahead of time and commit the exact number to memory.

Scripture Reference:
Hebrews 2:4

The Bread of Life

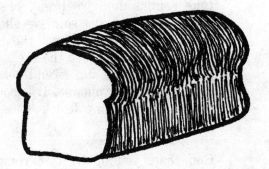

Motivation:	The leader displays a loaf of fresh, warm bread.
Activity:	The children are invited to touch and smell this bread as it is passed from child to child.
Guided Discussion:	How does this bread smell? (Wonderful. Good. Makes me hungry.) How does it feel? (Soft. Squishy.) Can we eat this bread just like this? (No.) What must we do? (Slice it. Cut it up into pieces.)
Leader Message:	A slice of bread is so common that sometimes we forget it was once a whole toasty brown loaf. We forget that it was carefully shaped from a large piece of dough and baked as a whole piece in an oven. Bread is an important part of our diet. That's why we don't just leave it whole and admire it and sniff it. Bread isn't much good unless it is used. A loaf is nice to look at,

but until it is sliced—until it is broken into smaller pieces—we can't use it. When we take communion, we break bread into small pieces. Jesus said we should remember him when we eat the bread of communion. It is when the bread of communion is broken and given to each of us that it becomes valuable. It becomes our way of remembering Jesus.

Closing
Prayer:

God, thank you for the joy of communion. As we break bread today, we remember and worship Jesus. Amen.

Materials:

A loaf of bread. It will be particularly effective if the loaf has been recently heated so as to feel warm and have a tantalizing aroma.

Scripture
Reference: John 6:35a

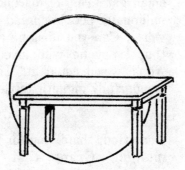

Your Table Is Waiting

Motivation: The leader displays a small, low table.

Activity: The children are invited to sit on the floor around this table.

Guided
Discussion: Is there room for everyone? (No.) How could we solve this problem? (Get more tables. Take turns. Get a bigger table.)

Leader
Message: Today we are celebrating worldwide communion. It is a day when, throughout the world, people who love Jesus come together to take communion. When we celebrate communion, we should remember that the first communion with Jesus and the disciples was held at a table. That table was much larger than this one, but it was not large enough to hold all the Christians who take communion today. Think of how the love of Jesus has grown from a

small gathering of disciples at a table to millions of people spread throughout the world. Can you imagine a table so large that everyone who loves Jesus in the whole world could fit? That would be a wonderfully gigantic table!

Closing
Prayer:

Dear God, thank you for the joy of communion. Grant that as we take communion today, we think of all the millions of Christians throughout the world who join with us in remembering Jesus. Amen.

Materials:

A small table. A play table, or other small, low table will do. It should be too small to accommodate all the children. In inviting the children to sit around the table, the leader should take care not to create a situation in which children will push and shove. If the congregation does not celebrate worldwide communion, the sermon can be modified to focus on the challenge of fitting all members of the congregation, plus Christians worldwide, around the small table. (The message, for example, could make the point that Christians throughout the world celebrate communion just as the local congregation does. The children could be invited to imagine how large the crowd would be if Christians everywhere joined the local congregation for communion.)

Scripture
Reference: Luke 13:24

Part One: The Fast Lane

Motivation: The leader displays a diagram of a car's
               instrument panel.

Activity: The children are invited to examine the
               diagram and think about what the various
               gauges and instruments tell the driver.

Guided
Discussion: Let's talk about what all these things do.
               Let's begin with this [point to fuel gauge].
               What does this tell us? (How much gas the
               car has. When we run out of gas.) [Con-
               tinue this process, pointing to various
               gauges. See the Materials section for a
               sample list of gauges.]

Leader
Message: I want to talk about a special gauge: the
               speedometer. Most of you know that the
               speedometer tells the driver how fast the
               car is going. The higher the number, the
               faster the car is traveling. All of our
               streets and roads have speed limits on
               them which tell us, "You can go this fast,
               but no faster." Speed limits have many

purposes, all related to safety. When people drive past your school on school days they must drive slowly and watch for children. When a car comes to a sharp curve, the driver must slow down to stay safely on the road. I wonder what would happen if people had speedometers and they had to obey speed limits. I'll bet a lot of speeding tickets would be issued. People run around at high speeds, going here and there, running errands, rushing, hurrying, speeding—especially during holiday times like Christmas and New Year's. Sometimes people, especially adults—but children too—need to be reminded not to speed through life. We all need to remember to slow down and take time to look around to view and appreciate God's wonderful world.

Closing
Prayer: God, we thank you for our wonderful world. Help us to slow down enough to appreciate everything you have provided. Amen.

Materials: A diagram representing a car's instrument panel. This can be roughly sketched on butcher paper or cardboard using one's own autombile instrument panel as a guide. Included might be the following: gas gauge, oil pressure gauge, radio dial, heater/air conditioner controls, voltage indicator, and temperature gauge. Some of these gauges are no longer standard equipment on today's modern computerized vehicles, but the gas gauge, radio dials, and heater/air conditioner controls will be fairly recognizable to children. Be certain to include, for this sermon, a speedometer and—in order to relate this sermon to "Part Two: How Fast, How Far?"—an odometer.

Scripture
Reference: Psalm 46:10a

Part Two: How Fast, How Far?

Motivation: The leader displays a diagram of a car's instrument panel.

Activity: The children are reminded that they have seen the diagram before. They are invited to examine the diagram and think about which gauges would be most helpful for a driver going on a long trip.

Guided
Discussion: Which of all these dials and buttons and gauges would be of most help to a driver going on a long trip, and why? (Various answers: The gas gauge, because the driver would need gas for a long trip. The radio, to help the driver to stay awake. The heater, in case it got cold. The speedometer, so the driver could keep track of the speed and not get a ticket. The odometer—mile counter—so the driver would know how far he or she has gone. And so on.)

Leader
Message: Let's talk some more about two very important gauges: the speedometer and the

odometer. Last time we determined that the speedometer tells the driver how fast the car is going. We also talked about how important it is to avoid speeding, both on the road and in living our lives. However, as we all begin a new year, it is important not only to know how fast we are going, but how far we have come. That's what the odometer on a car tells us. It records miles as they pass and totals them up for the driver to see. It tells the driver how far the car has gone. It is a very useful instrument. Now, of course, people like you and me don't have odometers to record our journeys through life. But we do have brains and hearts and memories. These are the instruments we use to record the events of our lives. So, as the new year begins, let us all take a moment to think about where we have been and where, with God's guidance, we will be going in the future.

Closing Prayer:

God, thank you for the precious gift of memory—our own personal odometer, our mileage counter—which helps us remember the blessings you have bestowed upon us in the past. We look forward to a future filled with your love and guidance. Amen.

Materials: See No. 31 "Part One: The Fast Lane" for details regarding materials.

Scripture Reference: 2 Corinthians 13:5a

Round and Round

Motivation: The leader displays a large piece of cardboard on which the letters *J, F, M, A, M,
J, J, A, S, O, N, D* are displayed in a circle
(see illustration).

Activity: The children are invited to study the illustration closely and to be prepared to
talk about it.

Guided
Discussion: Does anyone have an idea what this is?
(Various guesses. A game. A clock.) I'll
give you a hint. This *J* [point to the *J*]
stands for a month of the year. Any ideas?
[If the children recognize the diagram as a
calendar, or even if they still don't get it,
move on the the Leader Message.]

Leader
Message: Let's begin with this *J*. Now I want you to
join me in saying the names of the months
of the year in order, starting with January. [Go all the way through the letters—

January through December—pointing to each letter in turn as the children say the names of the months aloud.] You can see that this is a sort of calendar, with one letter representing each month. It shows one entire year, twelve months, arranged in a circle like a clock. You may have noticed, when we went around our clock calendar a few moments ago, how quickly a year passed. It's a funny thing about time. Children seem to want time to move more quickly. They are in a hurry to grow up. Adults seem to want time to move more slowly. They are in no hurry to grow old. And yet, the time passes. Time marches along just as we moved around our little calendar clock. An old year has just ended [or is just about to end] and a new year has just begun [or is about to begin]. And sooner than you think, January will speed by and then it will be spring and summer and fall and winter again. [The leader traces a circle from the *J* to the *D* to illustrate this portion of the message.] Round and round and round, time hurries by. We can't stop time and we can't go back, but we can be certain of one thing. Throughout each year, and throughout our lives, one thing never changes: God is always with us.

Closing
Prayer: Dear God, time passes so quickly. Thank you for remaining constant throughout our lives. Amen.

Materials: A large piece of cardboard with a circle of letters as shown in the illustration. The letters can be roughly spaced like the numerals on a clock face with the *D* (December) where the 12 would be, the *J* (January) where the 1 would be, and so on. The letters should be large enough to be seen by the children and, if possible, big enough so that a least some of the congregation can follow along. It may be helpful to display the cardboard on an easel to facilitate handling.

Scripture
Reference: Ephesians 5:14–16a

Part One: Yarn Yield

Motivation:　　　The leader displays several colorful pieces of yarn.

Activity:　　　Each child is asked to choose a piece of yarn.

Guided
Discussion:　　　What can we do with yarn? (Make things. Weave. Knit. Make sweaters and blankets.) Why did you choose the color you chose? (Like it. It's my favorite. It's pretty.) Did you expect that I would give you each a piece of yarn today? (No.) Was it a surprise? (Yes.)

Leader
Message:　　　It's wonderful to receive something, even a small present like these bright pieces of yarn. When the choice is to get something, or to give something up, most people will choose to get something. Most people are very reluctant to give things up. We Christians have just come through

[or are in the midst of] a period called Lent. Each year Lent starts on a special day known as Ash Wednesday, and it ends forty days later, on Easter Sunday. During Lent, Christians agree to give up or go without something as a way of saying they are sorry for things they have done wrong. Often we agree to go without something we like very much. Christians agree to do this because they have faith that other, greater rewards will follow if they are willing to give something up today. Now, I'm going to ask you each to give up something with a promise that—if you do—something very special will follow as we approach Easter. So, please, I want each of you to give me back the piece of yarn I gave you. [Leader collects all the yarn and places it in a bag.] Thank you. I hope you'll all join me again next time, and we'll talk some more about Lent and about Easter.

Closing
Prayer: God, help us to understand the importance of Lent. Help us to recognize the importance of our sacrifices. Help us to look forward with joy to the coming triumph of Easter. Amen.

Materials: Several bright-colored bits of yarn. A paper or plastic bag. Please note that this sermon is a companion activity with the two which follow. This triad begins with (or near the close of) Lent—reinforcing the sacrifices of that season—and continues with Palm Sunday, culminating on

Easter Sunday. The leader should carefully conduct this sermon's message and activity to ensure that children are not distressed by having to give up their yarn. When distributing yarn, for example, avoid such phrases as "This is yours" or "Here's one for you," since this tends to create an impression of ownership. See the Materials sections in Parts Two and Three for further details.

Scripture
Reference: Hebrews 13:15

Part Two: Pole Vault Preview

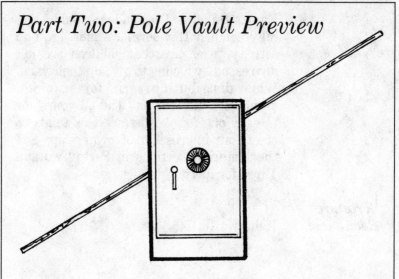

Motivation: The leader arrives carrying a long bamboo or fiberglass vaulting pole. Assistants also arrive carrying a small safe.

Activity: The children are invited to examine these items.

Guided Discussion: What is this pole used for? (Various answers. Fishing. High jumping. Pole vaulting.) How about this safe? (To keep things in. To put valuables in.)

Leader Message: A safe is sometimes called a *vault*. And, of course, this long pole can be used in a track and field event called the *pole vault*. So you might guess that the word "vault" is going to be very important in our message today. Let's talk about the pole first.

This pole is used to help an athlete rise into the air in order to jump over an obstacle: a crossbar placed way up high. Like this. [Show picture of an athlete pole vaulting.] It acts something like a large spring and a bit like a bow and arrow in giving the athlete a boost. Today is Palm Sunday. On this day long ago people were given a tremendous boost by taking part in a joyous parade like this. [Show appropriate illustration.] That parade celebrated Jesus' triumphant entry into Jerusalem. Now, you were correct about the safe. This vault contains something very valuable. Something that, when combined with our pole, forms a very precious thing. Between now and the next time we meet, I want you all to think about what might be in this vault. I'll give you a clue: it has something to do with the colorful pieces of yarn I asked you to give back to me last time. Think hard and share your guesses next time we get together.

Closing
Prayer:

God, we thank you for the special boost we get when we worship you. Thank you for lifting us higher and higher in pursuit of our goals. Thank you also for the safety your love provides. We look forward with joy to the celebration of Easter. Amen.

Materials:

A bamboo pole or a fiberglass vaulting pole, borrowed perhaps from the athletic department of a local school or from a sporting goods store. A bamboo pole might be best since, as a hollow pole will

91

be useful in Part Three of this sermon. A photo or drawing of an athlete pole vaulting, showing, ideally, the athlete, the pole, and the vaulting crossbar. An illustration showing Jesus' entry into Jerusalem. A small safe, perhaps borrowed from an office supply store. If one is not available, use a strongbox or metal box with a padlock. This sermon is the second of three parts and carries forward to the final segment a small "mystery." (Unknown to the children, the vault contains a special Easter banner which includes a fringe composed in part of yarn they held briefly in Part One.) If the leader feels the mystery might be too frustrating for the children, or that doing the sermon in three parts may endanger continuity, it might be best (although perhaps too ambitious) to do all three parts in one sitting. See the Materials sections for Parts One and Three for further details.

Scripture
Reference: Matthew 21:9–11

Part Three: Pole Vault Parade

Motivation:　　As in Part Two, the leader arrives carrying a long bamboo or fiberglass vaulting
pole. Assistants also arrive carrying a
small safe.

Activity:　　　The children are again invited to examine
these items.

Guided
Discussion:　　Last time we decided that this pole can be
used for pole vaulting and that this safe,
also called a vault, is used for storing valuable things. Remember, too, that last
time I asked you to think about what valuable thing might be kept in this vault. I
said it had something to do with those
colorful bits of yarn we passed around two
weeks ago. Any ideas? (Various guesses.
Given the leader's clue, some will probably say that the yarn is inside.)

Leader
Message:　　　God's word lifts us high over barriers,
much like this vaulting pole, and helps us
soar to new heights of love and joy. And
just as this pole lifts us high, a pole can be
used to lift high an important Easter message. Those of you who said the yarn was
inside the vault were partially correct.
Let's open the vault and see what we find.
[The leader unlocks the safe and pulls
forth a colorful banner. The banner can
carry one of several Easter messages:

"Christ is risen!" "Hosanna!" "Easter!" and so forth.] If you all look closely you'll see that those bits of yarn have joined with other colorful cloth to form this beautiful banner. Let's attach it to our pole. [The banner is affixed and raised to its full height. The leader may require some assistance from other adults.] Now there's a wonderful sight! I tell you what—remember that Palm Sunday parade we talked about last time? Let's have it right now! Here are some more bits of yarn for each of you to wave in the parade. [Pass these out.] I'll carry our large banner and you can follow me as I march through the parade route. [After a brief parade, the leader returns to the sermon site and secures the banner in a base.]

Closing
Prayer: Thank you, God, for the tremendous joy of Easter! Amen.

Materials: A bamboo pole or a fiberglass vaulting pole. See Part Two for details on how a pole might be obtained. A colorful banner. This might be commercially purchased or sewn by volunteers. Yarn similar to that handled by the children in Part One should be included in the banner, perhaps as a prominent fringe so that its presence is obvious to the children. An extra supply of yarn bits is also needed for the children to wave in the parade. It is important to prepare the pole and banner in advance so the latter can be easily and solidly affixed and to ensure that the pole

94

is sufficiently rigid to support the banner. A hollow bamboo pole may be preferred since a pin supporting the banner can be firmly inserted (see illustration). Make certain that the pole, when fully erected, will not collide with the ceiling or light fixtures. An appropriate base should be available in which the pole and banner can be secured. If possible, accompany the children's parade with appropriate stirring music and have the congregation stand and clap in time.

Scripture
Reference: Matthew 28:5–7

Flowers That Bloom in the Spring

Motivation: The leader displays a bouquet of flowers.

Activity: Each child is invited to select a flower.

Guided Discussion: [Leader addresses each question to a different child.] What color is your flower? (Yellow. Red. Other.) Do you know what kind of flower this is? (A daisy. A rose. Some will not know.) Why did you pick the flower you chose? (Liked the color. It was pretty.)

Leader Message: Each of these flowers is special and very beautiful. But each of you is even more special and more beautiful—so special that you have a name of your own. A flower can be known as a rose or a daisy, but did you ever meet a flower named

Mary? Or a rose named Billy? Let's each say our name and the group will repeat it. I'll begin. My name is _____. Now you all say, "_____." Good. Now [indicating a child], you say your name and we'll all say it back. [Repeat for all children.] Such beautiful names and such beautiful children! So far, we've been having all the fun up here. Let's let the rest of the congregation join in. When I count to three, I want each of you to walk to someone in the front row, hand that person your flower, and say your name. Then come right back here so we can watch what happens next. After you give your flowers away and say your names, the people who receive the flowers will turn around and hand them to people in the row behind them, introducing themselves as they do so. Then those people will hand the flowers to the people behind them and say their names, and so on. In this way our beautiful flowers and our beautiful names will travel all over the church. If they reach the last row, start passing them toward the front again, until the organ begins to play. Then we'll all stop for our closing prayer. Ready? One, two, three. Walk. [Allow the passing of the flowers to go on for a time. At a signal, the organist can play a short piece as a cue for the closing prayer.]

Closing
Prayer:

Dear God, thank you for all the wonderful, beautiful names by which we can come to know each other. Thank you for the opportunity to share our names and

97

ourselves with others. We pray in your holy name. Amen.

Materials: A variety of flowers, enough to give one to each child. Thorns and other prickles should be removed from stems. If supplying enough flowers for the whole group is impractical, the leader may assign some to stay up front and watch while others circulate the flowers. A variation is to have a child stand at each end of a row and pass the flowers in opposite directions, from person to person, to each other, as a collection plate might be passed. When the flowers reach the end of the rows, the children can bring them back and assemble at the front for the closing prayer. This variation has the advantage of allowing people to introduce themselves to those on either side of them.

Scripture
Reference: Matthew 18:20

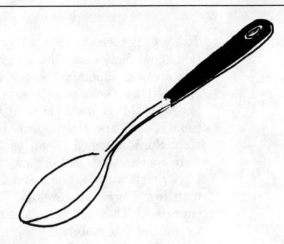

Steamed Up

Motivation: The leader displays a candle in a holder, a
                plastic container of water, a metal spoon
                with an insulated handle, and matches.

Activity: The children are invited to watch as the
                leader lights the candle, dips the spoon
                into the container and brings forth a small
                amount of water, then holds the spoon
                over the flame. The water in the heated
                spoon soon steams away. The leader blows
                out the candle, douses the hot spoon in
                the remaining water, and places all mate-
                rials aside.

Guided
Discussion: What happened to the water? (It disap-
                peared. Burned up. Steamed away. Evap-
                orated.) It started boiling and evaporated
                because of the flame. The water went into
                the air. Where is it now? (In the air. All
                around us.)

Leader Message: Today is Pentecost. It is a day when we talk about flames and fire, a day when we talk about change. Just as our water was changed by flame into steam, the followers of Jesus were changed by an encounter with the Holy Spirit. Before the Holy Spirit touched them, the followers were cold and flat, like our water. But the Holy Spirit warmed them and filled them with joy. They were excited! They were energized! They felt like floating! When we heated our water, it rose and joined with the air and floated all over the church. As you and I and everyone here breathed in the air, we were all touched by that steam. The followers were touched by the fire of the Holy Spirit, they were filled with the Spirit of God, and they went out and touched the world. Some followers wrote the words we read in the New Testament, words that have touched millions of lives—including yours and mine.

Closing Prayer: God, touch our hearts with your flame that we may be filled with the warmth of your Spirit. Grant that we may share our rejoicing spirit with those around us. Amen.

Materials: A candle securely mounted in a stable holder, a plastic container of water wide enough to allow the spoon to be inserted, a metal spoon with an insulated handle, and safety matches. The entire operation should take place on a stable, flat, non-flammable surface out of reach of the children. If the leader is concerned about using fire, this entire sermon can be adapted, using a cold tea kettle or a cold vaporizer as a prop, and asking the children what would happen if it were filled with water and heated. Another option is to show the children a picture of a steam engine spouting a steam cloud and to question them about how steam is caused and where it goes. If fire is used, the leader should be aware of the location of fire extinguishers or have an assistant nearby with an extinguisher in hand. A final consideration is whether the children will be influenced to try this activity at home. Since there is no real trick to the activity (the children have undoubtedly seen steam before) it is likely that most would not be tempted to duplicate it.

Scripture
Reference: Acts 2:1–21.

Part One: Clues to the Red, White, and Blue

Motivation: The leader displays an American flag.

Activity: The children are invited to study the flag and to be prepared to talk about its colors and shapes.

Guided Discussion: Our flag is a symbol. It represents our country. It stands for our nation. [Leader proceeds with the guided discussion indicating appropriate portions of the flag.] Let's talk about the stripes first. How many are there? (Thirteen. Seven red stripes. Six white stripes.) What do the stripes stand for? (The thirteen original colonies which became our first thirteen states.) What about the blue? (The blue field represents the sky.) How many stars are there? (Fifty.) What do the stars stand for? (Each star stands for a state of the union.)

Leader Message: June 14 is Flag Day, a day when we honor America's flag. We know a lot about our flag and we know a lot about our country. Our country and our flag are famous throughout the world. When most people look at our flag, they think of freedom, the freedom to speak and act and write and live our lives—and, of course, one of our most important freedoms, the one we're enjoying today: the freedom to worship.

Join me in honoring this flag that sym-
bolizes our special freedoms. Join me in
the Pledge of Allegiance. [The leader
stands, along with children and congregation, and all pledge allegiance to the
flag.]

Closing
Prayer: (If desired following the Pledge of Alle-
                  giance.) Dear God, thank you for the
                  freedoms we enjoy as Americans. We pray
                  that we may forever pledge our nation to
                  follow your holy way. Amen.

Materials: An American flag. One properly mounted
                  on a portable board and displayed on an
                  easel will be best for viewing and discus-
                  sion purposes. If time is a factor, the
                  leader might make the discussion period
                  go faster by asking, "What part of the flag
                  stands for the thirteen original colonies?"
                  "What part of the flag represents the blue
                  sky?" "What do the fifty stars stand for?"
                  or similar questions to which the children
                  can respond more readily.

Scripture
Reference: 2 Corinthians 3:17

Part Two: Flags from Afar

Motivation:　The leader displays the flag of another nation.

Activity:　The children are invited to look at this flag and to be prepared to answer questions about its colors and shapes.

Guided
Discussion:　Last week we celebrated Flag Day by studying our own American flag and discovered that we knew a great deal about the red, white, and blue colors and the stars and stripes. Today we are studying the flag of another nation: [state name]. Let's talk about the colors and shapes of this flag. [Leader asks questions like those in Part One. After children have ventured various opinions, the leader should tell them what certain colors and shapes mean.]

Leader Message:	(As noted in "Materials" below, this message may be adapted to fit various circumstances.) There are many, many countries in our world. As a result, there are also many, many flags, as well as many different languages, different kinds of clothing, different foods, and different holidays. But did you know that in nearly every country there are Christians? Jesus' love has spread throughout the world. When you next look at our American flag, think of the flags of other countries and of the millions of Christians in other countries around the world.
Closing Prayer:	Dear God, we join with Christians throughout the world in praising your holy name. Amen.
Materials:	Various approaches may be taken in preparing this sermon. The flag introduced could be one from a nation with which the congregation has a special relationship (missionary activities, relief efforts, and so on). The flag may be that of the home country of a visitor or new member of the congregation (for example, a foreign exchange student or a visiting pastor). The flag may also have regional significance, that of a neighboring nation. In some instances, it will be effective to have a person from the nation discuss with the children the significance of the flag. A source for a foreign flag can be a local flag or map store, an embassy or consulate, a

high school or college exchange student, a missionary, or a foreign church connection. Unless one can be assured of a faithful reproduction, it is *not* recommended that a flag be hand drawn. Resources for a detailed description of the significance of a given flag include an encyclopedia, an atlas, and other library reference books, plus, of course, a native of the country if such a person is available. As with the American flag displayed in Part One, it will be best to display the flag used in this sermon on a board. Make certain that such a display does not violate the concerned nation's patriotic protocol, and special care should be taken not to inadvertently display the flag upside down or backward. Above all, the leader should take pains to avoid all activities or statements which may demean another nation's flag.

Scripture
Reference: John 3:16a

Fireworks

Motivation: The leader asks the children to lie back and look up at the sanctuary ceiling.

Activity: The lights are dimmed and images of fireworks are projected on the ceiling, accompanied by appropriate sound effects (explosions, oohs and ahs). The children will probably chime in. After a few moments the lights are restored and the children are asked to sit up.

Guided Discussion:	Why do you suppose we are so excited about fireworks? (Loud. Colorful. Beautiful. Scary.) Why do we shoot off fireworks? (To celebrate the Fourth of July.)
Leader Message:	Each Fourth of July we see fireworks blazing in the night sky. This is one way to celebrate our nation's independence. We also display the flag, go on picnics, and watch or take part in parades. The Fourth is a big birthday party for America, but we sometimes forget the importance of what we are celebrating. In some parts of the world, explosions in the night are not happy events. In some places, bright lights in the sky mean shooting and fighting and war. And in many places, people are fighting one another over something which we in America already have: the freedom to worship. In America we are free to worship and to attend the church of our choice. Next time you see fireworks, remember how special our freedom is.
Closing Prayer:	God, thank you for the freedoms that our great nation provides. We are thankful especially that we are free to worship you. Amen.
Materials:	A slide projector and slides of fireworks. Possibly a projection screen if the ceiling or walls of the sanctuary do not lend themselves to reflecting a slide image. Fireworks slides might be obtained from a

souvenir shop or a professional or amateur photographer. An audiotape might be obtained from the sound effects collection of a local radio station. If the use of a slide projector is impractical, the audiotape alone could be used, the children being invited to imagine the fireworks that go with the sounds. If available, a videotape or movie of fireworks would also be effective. The children and the congregation might be encouraged to "ooh and ah" aloud when the fireworks are displayed.

Scripture
Reference: John 1:5

Point of View

Motivation: The leader arrives wearing sunglasses.

Activity: The leader announces to the children that this outfit is a Halloween costume.

Guided Discussion: What do you think of my Halloween costume? (It isn't enough. Not a real costume. You don't look any different except for the glasses.) What could I add to make a better costume? (A mask. Some funny clothes.)

Leader Message: Halloween means dressing up in fancy or scary or funny costumes. It's a fun time and a time when children can pretend. Some people pretend at other times. Sometimes they pretend so much they don't see things clearly. These glasses were designed to protect my eyes in the sun, but they can also distort the way I see things. Because of the special coloring in the sunglasses, I might see the world as either brighter or darker than it really is. My glasses might filter out reds or blues or yellows and make things appear different than they really are. The Bible and our religion help us see things clearly. They help us remove things that come between us and the real world, just as removing these glasses [does so] helps me clearly see and appreciate the true colors of this room and all your beautiful faces. The Bible offers us a clear vision, undisguised and true.

Closing
Prayer: God, thank you for the clear vision that the Bible provides. Thank you for bringing our world and our lives into sharp focus. Amen.

Materials: A pair of sunglasses. The kind that reflect or have an amber or other obvious tint may be particularly effective with children in making the point of altered vision.

Scripture
Reference: 1 Corinthians 13:12

Good News

Motivation: The leader displays a newspaper with a
               banner headline that reads: "EVERY-
               BODY VOTES."

Activity: The leader calls attention to the headline
               and, depending on the age of the children,
               either reads it aloud or asks for volunteers
               to read it for the group.

Guided
Discussion: What do you think this headline means?
               (That everybody voted.) Why do you think
               the fact that everyone voted deserves such
               a big headline? (Various answers. Because
               it means everyone took a turn. Everyone
               showed up.)

Leader Message: Every November, citizens of the United States have an opportunity to vote. Often we are criticized because a lot of us choose not to vote. The amount of people who vote in an election is called the *turnout*. If there is a low turnout, that is bad news; if there is a high turnout with a lot of people voting, that is good news, because it means people care and people are involved. So a headline that says, "Everybody Votes," is good news. The adults in our congregation can tell you that it isn't often these days that we read good news in the newspaper. Much of the news is bad, so a headline with good news is likely to get our attention. Here's another good news headline. [The leader now displays another newspaper (or an inside page of the same newspaper) with the headline, "EVERYBODY HEARS THE GOSPEL." As before, depending on the age of the group, the leader either reads it to them or has a volunteer read it aloud.] This is really, really good news. In fact, *gospel* means "good news." *Gospel* is a word we use to refer to the teachings of Jesus which, as we all know, contain lots and lots of good news. Each time we "turn out" to hear the teachings of Jesus—to hear the gospel—we are casting a vote for ourselves and for our relationship with Jesus. Let's hope that as each of you grow, you'll continue to help make this world a better place by voting in every election and by turning out to hear the gospel.

Closing
Prayer: Thank you, God, for caring so much about
                us that you sent Jesus to live and speak
                the Gospel. Thank you for the good news.
                Amen.

Materials: Two newspapers with headlines reading
                "EVERYBODY VOTES" and "EVERY-
                BODY HEARS THE GOSPEL," or a sin-
                gle newspaper with the former headline
                on the front page and the latter on an
                inside page. Special headlines can be
                handmade by using transfer letters or by
                hand printing, pasting, or taping the let-
                ters onto a regular newspaper, or they can
                be specially produced at a local print shop
                or gift store. It may be particularly effec-
                tive to use a local newspaper familiar to
                the children.

Scripture
Reference: Luke 4:17b–18b

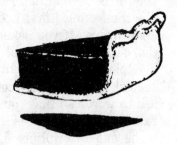

A Question of Taste

Motivation: The leader displays a pumpkin pie.

Activity: The children are invited to think about how pumpkin pie tastes.

Guided
Discussion: What does pumpkin pie taste like? (The children will probably have trouble expressing this. Some may say, "Like a pumpkin" or "Like pie." Be prepared for some to say they dislike the taste.)

Leader
Message: Whether you think it tastes wonderfully or "yucky," it is difficult to describe the taste of pumpkin pie, isn't it? Soon it will be Thanksgiving Day, and at my house pumpkin pie is always a big part of the feast. I enjoy it. I look forward to it. But, do you know, I seldom stop to think exactly what it tastes like, even when I'm eating it. It is a question, in fact, that I don't think I could answer very well even if I did think about it. The taste of pumpkin pie can't be described. It is indescrib-

able; it is beyond description. It's sort of like the feeling I first had when I came to know Jesus. If you asked me to describe that feeling, I could tell you it was exciting, pleasant, wonderful, and very, very special, but I probably couldn't totally put it into words so that you would know just exactly how I felt. It is so wonderful as to be beyond description. All I can really say is, when Thanksgiving comes around every year, I am so very, very thankful that I know Jesus!

Closing Prayer: Dear God, I give thanks that I know Jesus. Though words fail me, help me to communicate to others the joy I feel. Amen.

Materials: A pumpkin pie. Depending upon the leader's knowledge of the children's dietary restrictions and the decorum of the setting, the pie might be divided and eaten either at the sermon site or elsewhere following the sermon.

Scripture Reference: Psalm 100:4–5

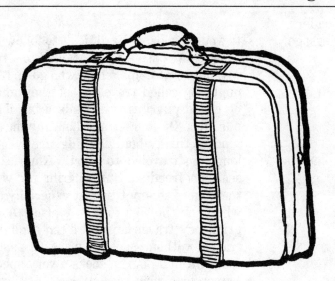

Pilgrim Pathways

Motivation: The leader displays a small suitcase.

Activity: The children are told that the leader is about to leave on a trip. They are invited to come along and are instructed to follow the leader on a brief journey around the sanctuary. The leader, the children in tow, weaves about in a fairly complicated pattern and then returns to the meeting area.

Guided
Discussion: Where did our little trip begin? (Here. Where we are now.) And where did we end up? (Here again.) Do you think you could take that trip again, exactly the same way we went? (Some will say yes; some no.)

Leader Message: It would probably be difficult to follow the exact same path we just walked together without some help. People who go on trips might be called travelers, or they might be called pilgrims. Let's talk a bit about pilgrims. Of course, at Thanksgiving we tend to think about *the* Pilgrims who so long ago traveled to North America in search of freedom. But "pilgrim" is a word that refers to any traveler, especially one who is on the way to a holy place. A pilgrim may travel far, and often a pilgrim travels without such luxuries as a suitcase. Often a pilgrim seeks a very special person or a very special place. A pilgrim often travels in search of knowledge. Along the journey, a pilgrim may be helped by people who show the way, or who offer encouragement. If a pilgrim is lost, someone may come and point out the trail. If a pilgrim is thirsty, someone may offer water. A pilgrim may travel alone, but a pilgrim may make many new friends on the way. Our little journey around the church could be called a pilgrimage—a pilgrim's journey. In the same way, our journey *to* church each Sunday might be called a pilgrimage. We come to this holy and special place seeking knowledge. And here we find many people to help us: our minister, our teachers, our choir, our organist, the ushers, the church secretary, the custodians, and everyone in our congregation. [The leader addresses the children] Welcome, pilgrims! Welcome to the exciting journey in search of God.

Closing
Prayer: Dear God, we thank you for the journey of life. Thank you also for those who help us along our way. Pilgrims that we are, we seek to come closer to you. Amen.

Materials: A small suitcase or perhaps a backpack.

Scripture
Reference: Matthew 24:44

Sign Here

Motivation: Shortly after the leader and the children gather together, a delivery person arrives with a package.

Activity: The leader signs for the package, and the delivery person departs.

Guided
Discussion: Unusual packages have begun arriving at our house. Any unusual packages at your homes yet? (Yes. No.) This one says, "Don't open until Christmas." Why must I wait? (You have to wait to open packages on Christmas. It's a rule. Opening them early would spoil the surprise. Santa wouldn't like it.) Any ideas what might be inside? (Various guesses.)

Leader
Message: Today is the First Sunday of Advent. Advent is a period of four Sundays before Christmas when we begin to look forward to celebrating the birth of Jesus. Have you ever noticed that the word "advent" forms the first six letters in the word "adventure"? An adventure is an exciting experience, and that's certainly what Advent is all about. We don't know yet what's inside all the packages that begin to appear around this time of year, but we do know that something good is inside. The feeling of Advent is like the excitement we feel when we think about what might be in a Christmas package. We know something good is going to happen this Christmas season. And we know that in addition to the wonderful presents we receive, the very best gift of all will be celebrated on Christmas Day: the reality of Jesus.

Closing
Prayer: Dear God, we thank you for the birth of Jesus. We look forward with joy to the Christmas celebration. Advent is a special time for us all to experience the wonderful waiting which leads to Jesus. Amen.

Materials: A plainly wrapped package and an assistant to pose as a delivery person. On the package write the words "Do Not Open Until Christmas" boldly.

Scripture
Reference. Luke 1:67–79

121

Luck of the Draw

Motivation: The leader displays a large plastic jar containing small envelopes.

Activity: The leader invites the children to speculate about what uses this combination could serve.

Guided Discussion: What could we do with this jar and these envelopes? (Various guesses. Children will likely be confused. Some may specualte that it's a game or a drawing for a prize of some sort.)

Leader Message: Today is the Second Sunday of Advent, a season of joyous waiting for Christmas. When I was little, we used to have Christmas name drawings. In a name drawing you write everyone's name on a small slip of paper and place each slip in an envelope. Next, you place the envelopes in a container like this jar. Then everyone gathers around and reaches in. If I reach in and pull out your name, that means I have to get you a special gift. If you get my name, then you must get me a special gift. Part of the fun is that you don't know whose name you are going to get and you don't know who will get your name. Remember, we are still in that season of the year known as Advent. This Sunday is part of the adventure of Advent: the wonderful waiting for Christmas. Now, since you have all been waiting so patiently, let's have each of you draw a name. As I come around to you, I'd like each of you to reach in and draw out an envelope, but let's wait and open them all together. [Leader allows each child in turn to draw an envelope, reminding each not to open it yet. When each child has an envelope, the leader also takes one and places the jar to one side.] All right, now let's all open our envelopes and see whose name is inside. [All slips of paper say "Jesus." The children will probably share this out loud.] My goodness, I wonder what sort of special gift we could all give to Jesus. The answer is, we can give ourselves. Now, who do you suppose has your name? (Various guesses.) All of you have Jesus' name, so Jesus must have your name. Just think of what special people you all are to exchange gifts with Jesus.

Closing Prayer:	Dear Jesus, thank you for calling us to give ourselves to you, and thank you for the gift of life you give us in return. Amen.
Materials:	A large plastic jar and sufficient envelopes and slips of paper to ensure that each child and the leader can draw one. "Jesus" should be written on each slip of paper. If envelopes are impractical, slips of paper folded over can be used. Envelopes are better, however, since they obscure the surprise and help ensure that the children all read the slips at the same time.
Scripture *Reference:*	Matthew 1:21

Odds and Ends

Motivation: The leader displays an odd-shaped package wrapped in Christmas paper (it contains a not too well disguised bicycle).

Activity: The children are invited to examine carefully the package and guess what might be inside.

Guided
Discussion: What do you think might be inside this package? (Various guesses including, probably, the correct one: a bicycle) Why do you think it's a bicycle? (You can tell by the shape.)

Leader
Message: Today is the Third Sunday of Advent. With each Advent Sunday, we get closer and closer to Christmas, the day we celebrate the birth of Jesus. Remember that Advent is an adventure of wonderful waiting. If we pinch and poke and shake our packages, or sometimes if we just study the shape, we can guess what's inside. But even then, we must wait to open it. Let's go back to our package. We have guessed, correctly, that there's a bicycle inside. We know it's a bike, but we don't know yet what color it is. And we can't yet predict every single thing we'll do when we open it and go for a ride. So even though we know it's a bicycle, there are still many surprises and many adventures we can't predict. Christmas is both an adventure

and a never-ending surprise. We know things will happen—wonderful things—but we really only have hints about what Christmas will mean this year and how it will change our lives in the future.

Closing
Prayer:

Dear God, your world is full of surprises. Even though we glimpse a bit of the future, you have even more wonderful adventures in store for us than we can possibly imagine. We look forward with joy to the coming of Christmas. Amen.

Materials:

A fully wrapped bicycle. It should be obvious from the shape that it is a bicycle (see illustration).

*Scripture
Reference:*

1 Corinthians 7:7

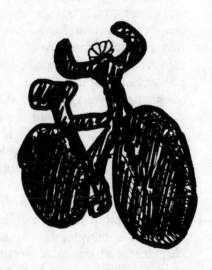

A Gift for All Occasions

Motivation: The leader displays a single wrapped package that has a large tag on it which says: "Open Before, During, and After Christmas."

Activity: The children are invited to examine the package and the tag.

Guided Discussion: What does this tag say? [Depending on the age of the children, the leader may have a volunteer read the tag aloud or may read it for them: "Open Before, During, and After Christmas."] How is this different from the tags we usually see on Christmas packages? (Usually the tag says, "Do Not Open *Before* Christmas.")

Leader Message:	Today is the Fourth Sunday of Advent. We have waited patiently during this exciting time before Christmas, and now that joyful day is nearly here. Usually the tags on our presents remind us not to open our packages *before* Christmas. And yet here is a tag that says, "Open Before, During, and After Christmas." I wonder what sort of gift this is which says it should be opened all year round. As far as I can see [the leader holds the package this way and that, examining it from various angles] there is only one way to discover what's inside, and that's to follow the instructions. Shall we? (Yes!) All right. [The leader carefully unwraps the package to reveal a Bible.] Now here's a gift for all occasions. Here's a gift we should open all year round. We should open the Bible throughout the year to receive all the gifts that God intended. Let's open this Bible, and I will read for you the Lord's Prayer. As I read, I would like you and the members of the congregation to join me in saying this wonderful prayer.
Closing Prayer:	The Lord's Prayer.
Materials:	A Bible wrapped in colorful Christmas paper. A prominent tag reading, "Open Before, During, and After Christmas."
Scripture Reference:	Matthew 6:9–13

Cookie Clues

Motivation: The leader displays a collection of cookie-baking equipment and ingredients.

Activity: The children are invited to examine these items and to be prepared to discuss their uses.

Guided Discussion: You're all good detectives. What do you make of these clues? What are these things used for? (Various guesses. To cook with. To make cookies.)

Leader Message: It's Christmas. Throughout Advent we have been talking about the weeks leading up to Christmas as an adventure, an exciting experience filled with wonder and waiting. And now Christmas is here at last. It's sort of like waiting for someone to get all the things together to bake cookies. First the ingredients have to be assembled, then the pots and pans and spoons and mixing bowls and measuring cups have to be found. Next there's the mixing, then everything goes in the oven, and then—while we're waiting for the cookies to bake—everything has to be cleaned up. It seems as though it takes forever, and all the time we are getting hungrier and hungrier, especially when we smell those yummy cookies baking! That feeling of waiting is called *anticipation*. It is the feeling of Advent. Finally, the cookies are ready and we get to eat them. Yum! That feeling is like the feeling of Christmas. Now, did you really think I was going to talk about making cookies without offering you some? First let us give thanks. [After the prayer, the leader distributes a cookie to each child.]

Closing
Prayer:

Dear God, thank you for the joyous Christmas season. Thank you for rewarding our patient waiting with the wonderful news of Jesus' birth. Amen.

Materials:

Cookie-baking supplies: flour, sugar, an egg (hardboiled for safety), cookie cutters, a cookie sheet, a rolling pin, a mixing bowl, spoons, measuring cups, and so forth. It will probably be most convenient to have these assembled in a basket or already in place on a table under a cover so that time is not taken in setting up the display. Previously baked cookies to distribute. Ideally these should be from a low sugar or sugar substitute (for instance, honey) recipe, and each should be individually wrapped in clear plastic for good hygiene. Plain butter cookies will probably be sufficient. The leader should determine whether it is better to distribute cookies at the close of the sermon or later.

Scripture
Reference:

Luke 2:9–11

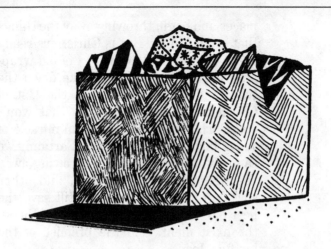

All Wrapped Up

Motivation:	The leader displays a box of used, torn, and crumpled wrapping paper.
Activity:	The children are invited to examine the box and its contents.
Guided Discussion:	What's in my box? (Old paper. used wrapping paper. Trash. Junk.) Is it any good anymore? (No. All torn.)
Leader Message:	Christmas is over for another year, and although there are lots of new things at your house, there are also lots of left-overs: crumpled wrapping paper, leftover Christmas dinner, and maybe a Christmas tree that will have to come down someday soon. When Christmas is over, we usually put all our new shiny gifts into special

places and begin throwing away the things that are left over. But is Christmas really over? When I throw this box of old wrapping paper away, when I take down the tree, and when I finish up the last of Christmas dinner leftovers, that won't end Christmas. The wonderful miracle of Jesus' birth will still be true. Certainly we can tidy up our homes by throwing away the wrappers, the old tags, and other such leftovers, but we can still save the best part of Christmas: the joy, the hope, the excitement, and the promise of the birth of Jesus.

Closing
Prayer: Dear God, we thank you for the chance to celebrate the birth of Jesus. Grant that we may celebrate the blessing of Christmas all year long. Amen.

Materials: A box containing obviously crumpled and torn Christmas wrapping paper.

Scripture
Reference: 2 Peter 3:8

New and Used

Motivation: The leader produes a variety of obviously well-worn toys.

Activity: The children are invited to examine the toys.

Guided Discussion: What's wrong with these toys? (They're broken. No good anymore. Need to be fixed.)

Leader Message: Each Christmas children like you receive wonderful toys and other gifts. A few days or weeks later we are unhappy to discover that one or two or more of these wonderful things are broken. Sometimes they can be repaired, and sometimes they are so badly damaged they need to be thrown away. This makes us sad for a time, but we usually get over it; besides, there are more toys coming for birthdays and for next Christmas. You know, this business of breaking sometimes happens to other things besides toys, especially to an important thing we call the *spirit*. We have all heard of the Christmas spirit. During Christmas we are supposed to be happy and love each other and care about each other. But when Christmas is over, we sometimes lose the Christmas spirit. That spirit gets broken down by problems and worries and, before you know it, we are sad or we do something mean. All because our spirit is broken. Let's all work hard to keep our spirits up and to lift the spirits of others, not just during Christmas, but all year round.

Closing
Prayer: Dear God, we are like these toys. We are fragile and sometimes we feel broken and mistreated. Restore our spirits and make us instruments of healing. Amen.

Materials: A few badly broken toys (a squashed truck, for example, or a ball with a gash in it or a wagon with a bent wheel). Be careful that the damaged goods do not have sharp edges. It might be effective to wrap a damaged toy in a mangled box and unwrap it to reveal the broken contents. Care should be taken to avoid frustrating children by displaying broken toys since some (perhaps those who got no toys at all) may say something like, "I'll take it" or "Don't toss it out, I want it" or "Why did you break that? I'd have taken it." If the leader has any inkling that some children may be frustrated by the broken toy display, he or she should substitute an adult gift like a phonograph record that could be shown to be broken. A broken record might be accompanied by a story about someone having sat on it.

Scripture
Reference: Ecclesiastes 3:1, 3b